The Right Way to Coach Football

A Football Coaching Guide

By

Coral (C.J.) Lambert

1663 Liberty Drive, Suite 200
Bloomington, Indiana 47403
(800) 839-8640
www.AuthorHouse.com

© 2005 Coral (C.J.) Lambert. All Rights Reserved.

No part of this book may be reproduced, stored in a retrieval system, or transmitted by any means without the written permission of the author.

First published by AuthorHouse 07/05/05

ISBN: 1-4208-6412-2 (sc)

Printed in the United States of America
Bloomington, Indiana

This book is printed on acid-free paper.

THE RIGHT WAY TO COACH FOOTBALL

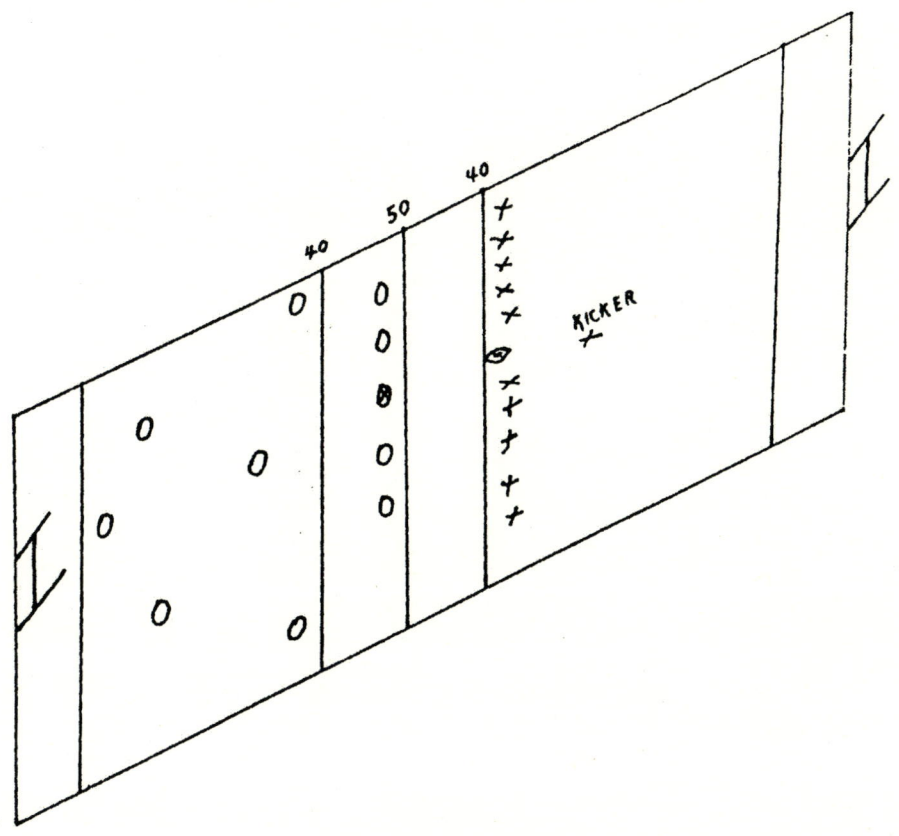

BY C. J. LAMBERT

TABLE OF CONTENTS

PRECIS ix

INTRODUCTION xi

PHILOSOPHY 1

STRATEGY 2

PRACTICE SCHEDULE 5

    FIRST FOUR WEEKS 5

THE SCOUTING REPORT 8

    SCOUTING THE OFFENSE 8

    DEFENSIVE SCOUTING 8

OFFENSE 10

    HUDDLE FORMATION 10

    RUNNING PLAYS 13

    SPECIAL PLAYS 14

    FLY SERIES 16

    SERIES PLAYS 17

    CROSS OR X BUCK SERIES 17

    TRIPLE OPTION SERIES 18

    BLOCKING RULES 21

    PASSING PLAYS OTHER THAN PLAY ACTION 22

DEFENSE 27

    5 - 4 ZONES FOR DEFENSIVE BACKS 31

    5 – 4 CORNERBACKS 32

    5 - 4 ZONE FOR LINEBACKERS 32

5 - 4 MAN TO MAN	33
VICTORY DEFENSE	37
KICKING GAME	41
SUMMARY	45

PRECIS

This Precis is about a football coaching system that can be used to help one become a successful coach. It is entitled <u>The Right Way To Coach Football</u>. This booklet is written with the assumption that the reader has some knowledge of football. This directive is very much needed by colleges and universities throughout the country. I have first-hand knowledge of this because I have coached ten years at nine junior and senior high schools throughout Louisiana, and I have attended many coaching conventions held by coaches from different regions of the country. I also played four years of collegiate football at Southeastern Louisiana University, Hammond, Louisiana.

The booklet is concise but thorough, and it focuses on the right way to get the job done, Philosophy and strategy are explained in a simple manner, and if followed will underline the innermost aspects of the young adolescent.

It is very important to pay close attention to the safety part of the game. This is overlooked by many coaches. The booklet explains the type of conditioning to use in order to protect joints and tissues of the skeleton system. This system keeps football on a game level and still encourages hard work and leadership. Injured players are ridiculed by many coaches. A simple rule is to treat every injury even small ones, and always have a first aid kit handy. Use a humanistic approach to coaching, and follow the golden rule, treat a person as you would want to be treated.

When planning a program, make it suitable to the type of players that you have, using size and speed of individuals as a criteria. Plan plays for each game and save some plays for important games. Play all players and keep the team happy. Never degrade a student in front of his peers. Use a balanced attack of passing and running plays, and let the quarterback run the offense because he is usually intelligent, and this teaches leadership. It is easy to put in a multiple look offense and a man-to-man defense that will not fail. All of these aspects are covered in the booklet along with the kicking game. I think you will agree with me that this endeavor is much needed because our young are our most important resource. Young coaching hopefuls need this message so that they are not brain-washed by the old methods that hurt the young mentally and physically. The booklet contains fifty-five hundred words and many illustrations.

       Author,
      Coral J. Lambert

INTRODUCTION

This booklet is compiled with the expressed purpose of giving college graduates or experienced coaches a briefing on football coaching. This booklet is written with the assumption that the reader has some knowledge of football. It contains valuable information compiled through ten years of coaching experience. This composition can give direction to any coach who needs it, especially to college hopefuls. It is also hoped that it can one day be used as a collegiate teaching tool for colleges and universities. There is no other simplified version of this type to my knowledge, and I have all the confidence in the world that by studying this pamphlet a coach will become a better coach and he will have a clear cut plan to follow if he chooses this system.

PHILOSOPHY

Most coaches have been brained-washed into thinking that winning is everything, and this leads them into forgetting that junior and senior high school students are still young adults that want to have fun. I would like to instill a philosophy that lets students enjoy themselves while learning team work, hard work, and sportsmanship.

From the beginning a coach should teach leadership by using positive words to his players. Words such as "kill; destroy' take his head off; kick butt' break his arm off and beat him in the head with it," and vulgarity should be eliminated completely. The coach should point out the dangers of football and let the team know that there is room for injury in the sport. A fact to point out is that football is a high impact sport, and proper technique will be taught and demanded. An example of this is that of sliding the head gear to one side or the other when blocking or tackling.

Be sure that when a player is hurt that he is not ridiculed. This will cause players to be at ease about reporting all injuries, no matter how minor they may be. Players should be taught to hit hard, but never hit anyone from the blind side. The team will take on the attitude of the head coach, and it must be a leadership role.

It should go without saying that a coach should not ridicule a player in front of his peers, but this is a common practice. Name-calling is also a practice that is used; it too is totally unnecessary. Coaches should never hit or kick any player, not even lightly. Such an act is very demoralizing to a youngster. The players should know the coach respects them as young adults, and they will respect him in return.

Coaching today's youth is a vitally important job because it gives the youth standards, goals, and positive habits. These must be in correct form because many football players take leadership roles in our society. The young heart is tender and should be treated accordingly; the young body is strong and quick, and should be worked to its fullest potential without permanent damage to joints and tissues. Coaches should be men and not child abusers. The next section on strategy will expound this phase of coaching philosophy.

STRATEGY

The first and most important strategy is to get players physically conditioned. Most coaches don't have a pre-conditioning program. I will mention the basics of one now. The most important part of the football player is the joints, and these must be strengthened. Coaches should stress summer activities such as swimming, bicycling, and weight lifting. Jogging is not good for the ankle and knee joints, and should be avoided. Weight lifting should be used for strength building and not simple muscle tone. This is accomplished by fewer repetitions, (3-5) and more weight on the bar. The first two weeks of practice should have an abundance of stadium runs and stretching exercises. Coaches should check knees by having players lie on their backs and lift one leg at a time to a ninety degree position. If the leg cannot be stretched out straight, then the knee needs to be strengthened. Building good knee muscle is of vital importance, and stadium or stair running is excellent for this.

A coach should cut his team down, but a quad A school could keep forty-four players and use every one of them. Some smaller players should be influenced into other sports, especially track. A school should have a track program; this builds athletes for all sports.

If possible, players should be placed at a position immediately and designate the teams by names and not by first offense, etc. Examples are school colors: gold offense, green offense, gold defense, green defense. Avoid letting a team know the first string is sacked up, especially in the early games. It is easy to establish two offenses and two defenses if a team has forty-four players or there can be players on two or more teams. Simply let the second team watch the first team perform a play, and then let the second team run it immediately. After both teams know enough plays, switch them around so that they are not sure which is first string. As the weeks go by, the best players will be sorted and put on the dominant team.

It is important that the coach keep the whole team happy and not just the top eleven. To do this is simple. First, let the so-called second defense play in the game when the opponents have the ball in their territory. Let the second offense play when the ball is between the forties, or if they are driving, let them continue. Most coaches will be shocked at the good effort second teams will deliver. I know, because I have tried this at both small and large schools. It also helps to place people that don't play much on special teams. Teams such as kick off returns, punt and punt returns, and extra points are of great importance in a game, and these should be worked on a little each day.

At practice, it is important to work on each facet of the game every day, and it is important not to have game situation scrimmages most of the time. An example of this is: before practice, assign a coach to work with the kicking game. In practice this is valuable time wasted that can help win games. During scrimmages, arrange to have only certain parts of the defense go full speed; such as only down linemen, only linebackers, or only defensive backs. This will allow the coach to see how well each row of defense plays against various offenses. The offense is always full speed in a scrimmage of this type. The coach can run a running play and let only defensive backs go live to see if they can react to the run and the coach can do the same for the other sections. This will prevent a lot of injuries and show the coach who can play and who cannot play defense. A practice schedule will be shown in the next section.

When preparing plays for the games, always pick out a series of plays for each opponent after you have found their weaknesses. With this series, work on a special play that won't be run until an important district game. These play series will be covered in a later section. Most plays can be run from different formations. This will be illustrated in the offensive section of the book. Always have short yardage and goal line offenses well versed and let the quarterback call the whole series. This teaches him leadership. Linemen should be foot to foot on these plays and wedge blocking will be used. The count shall always be on the second count or more for short yardage plays and one end will always split out to see how the defense covers him. If he could be open, the quarterback will call an audible and throw to him; otherwise a straight hand off will be run. Audibles are covered under the offensive portion of this booklet.

Defense will be man to man in most of the plays, and each position will be taught responsibilities, daily. Stunting will be done on special occasions, like goal line or long yardage plays. Keys will be explained on the defensive section of this booklet.

It is a good practice not to let linemen block downfield on running plays. This immediately telegraphs a run to the defensive back and he can come up with reckless abandon. On every pass play there should always be a release man to the sidelines in case all receivers are covered. If another quarterback is going to be used, be sure his personal center snaps to him on the sideline and both players go into the game.

Always set up the offenses and defenses to suit the player's ability. Examples are as follows: If there are many down linemen type, then use a six man front defense. If you have many small linemen type, use a four-four to hide linebackers. The same arrangement can be made on offense. If there are small, fast people, the team should throw a lot more. Running and passing balance is important if the team is going to win championships.

PRACTICE SCHEDULE

This is a short, fast-pace schedule. Coaches must stress quickness and agility. Remember repetition is the key to learning. Therefore, do the same drills daily, and be sure to cover every phase of the game daily. Also, have kickers, ball holders, receivers and passers warm up before the practice starts. A coach should be on the field fifteen minutes early every day for this purpose. Coaches should alternate this position.

FIRST FOUR WEEKS

3:00 – 3:10 Warm-up
Do a lot of stretching (examples: hurdle stretch, leg lifts, push ups).

3:10 – 3:30 Agility
Divide the team among four coaches (the head coach can rotate). Coach A – Tire drill as follows: Line up ten tires. Run players through rapidly in bear walk position, at the end of the tenth tire the player will hit a dummy, switch dummy holder periodically. Stress quickness and one hundred percent effort. All drills must be short and quick. A diagram is shown on the following page.

Coral (C.J.) Lambert

{DIAGRAM OF FOUR TIRE CYCLES}

```
DUMMY        DUMMY        DUMMY        DUMMY

 ⦿           ɪⓘ           ɪOɪ          ɪOɪ
 ɪ            ɪ            ɪ            ɪ
 ɪ            ɪ            ɪ            ɪ
 ɪ            ɪ            ɪ            ɪ
 ɪ            ɪ            ɪ            ɪ
 ɪ            ɪ            ɪ            ɪ

 ⦿           ɪⓘ           ɪOɪ          ɪOɪ
 ⦿           ⓘɪ            ⦿           ɪOɪ
 ⦿           ɪⓘ           ɪOɪ          ɪOɪ
 ⦿    ↑      ⓘɪ            ⦿           ɪOɪ
 1            2            3            4        ɪ = FOOT
```

Cycle 1 – Both feet in tires

Cycle 2 – Alternate feet, left foot in then right foot in on the next tire.

Cycle 3 – Alternate both feet in, then both feet out on the next tire.

Cycle 4 – Both feet out on each side of tires all the way through ten tires.

Hands are always placed on the next tire for balance as in bear walking.

Because humans are erect, this exercise is very important. It is important that the body stay low in most football techniques.

Coach B – (1) Hitting seven man sled or hand dummies with the right and left forearm, (2) hand shivers, (3) six point stance and fire out (hands, knees and feet touching the ground at the start of the fire out.) Always have a dummy holder at the end of the sled for each person to fire into at the end of the drill.

Coach C – Grass drills – players will do seat rolls, over and under, bear walk, knee planting drill, and push up drills. The drills in this workout will be done by the team members following the direction of movement given by the coach with a football in his hand. Directions are right, left, up, or down.

Coach D – Sideline tackling – stress: head gear across the body of the ball carrier, and don't over-run the ball carrier.

These drills may be changed if coaches know other good ones to use. The above are very easy to put in, but any more explanations would have to be demonstrations which could be arranged if needed.

On the above drills, it is a good idea to have four teams picked that will stay together throughout this time period. Then all linemen will go to two coaches, and all backs will go to two coaches for the next phase of the practice.

3:30 – 4:00 - - Offense and Defense

Linemen will work on offensive blocking and defensive technique against each other. Backs will work on ball handling and pass defense against each other. After fifteen minutes, defense will get on offense and offense on defense.

4:00 – 4:30 - - Team Scrimmages

Use fifteen minutes for each team, and use certain rows of the defense for live play scrimmage against opponents. The kicking game will be covered at the end of each of these sessions. Also during this time scouting material will be covered.

4:30 – 4:45 - - Conditioning

Stadium runs or sprints are important. Many people use their own system.

After four weeks of this schedule, the team should be ready for a slower pace, and should be given days off from sprints if the practice goes well. Alternate days when either agility or sprints are skipped. As the season goes on and there is no chance for a play off berth, start using the players for next year without eliminating seniors, completely. Give these players a lot of game experience. Always try to have two offenses and two defenses that can play well, even though some players may be on two teams.

THE SCOUTING REPORT

A good scouter should get to the game early so that he can get an idea on the team's organization. The scouter should get the starting line ups of the offense and defense, the weights of each person, and the age of each person.

SCOUTING THE OFFENSE

A form such as the following can be used to jot down each formation, plays ran, and also the down and position on the field.

Diagram each play as they occur, then compile the results to find out the team's tendencies. This may be done for more than one game by using films. Go over these at scrimmage practice. Be sure to note how the defense was aligned for the particular game. If the same play is run on the same formation and down, you may make a mark on the diagram already drawn.

DEFENSIVE SCOUTING

It is very important to stand on the end zone line to get the exact alignment of the defensive game and to watch for stunts. Be sure to draw the different defenses used, and the estimated percentage of the game it was used. Many coaches have their own detailed scouting forms, so there will not be any more discussion of this topic. If a team is well coached, they will be able to perform well against any defense or offense in games. This brings us to the next section, which illustrates how to function against various sets.

{EXAMPLES OF SCOUTING FORM}

Down 1 + __10__
yd. Ln. + or ⊖ __35__
Position Rt. Lt. (mid)

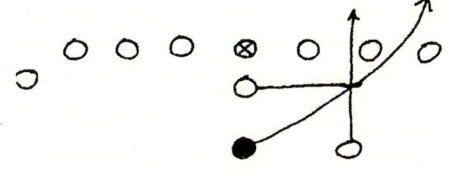

Down 2 + ____
yd. Ln. + or - ____
Position Rt. Lt. mid

Down 3 + ____
yd. Ln. + or - ____
Position Rt. Lt. mid

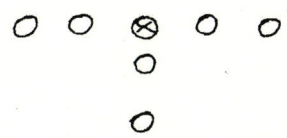

Down 4 + ____
yd. Ln. + or - ____
Position Rt. Lt. mid

OFFENSE

This offense is a multi-look offense and features simplicity by drilling quarterbacks into calling plays that will direct the entire team. The offense will be run in a series of plays. Many plays can be run from all formations. A scouting report will not help the opponents because different series and formations will be used in each game. The quarterback calls the formation right or left, the play with the hole number and the back number, and the series right or left. The two-digit number tells the back number and the hole number of the play. (Example: 34 – 3 is the fullback and 4 is the hole number.)

A few examples of calls by quarterbacks are as follows:
(A) Power I right, 34 slant right.
(B) Strong slot right, 46 cross buck left.
(C) Strong pro left, 38 cross buck left.

Next, the quarterback gives the count as follows: down, set, 85, hike, hike. The count is any of these sounds and a third hike may be added. Eighty-five can be any number, but there will be live numbers that will represent audibles. As soon as the lineman gets to the line of scrimmage, they must be in a three point stance, ready to go on down.

The huddle should be seven yards from the football; this distance saves energy for the offensive team.

HUDDLE FORMATION
{LINE OF SCRIMMAGE}

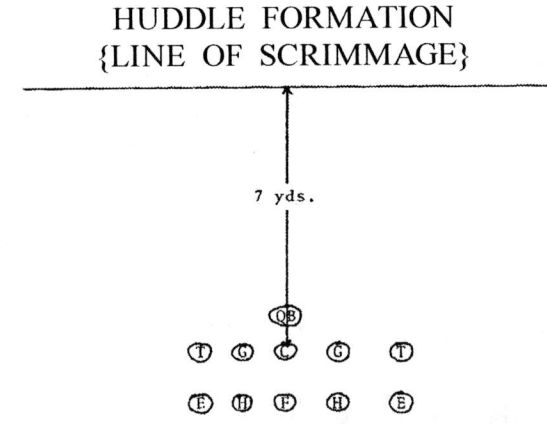

{THIS ROW IS STANDING.}
{THIS ROW HAS HANDS ON THEIR KNEES.}

The quarterback calls the play and the count and steps aside for the center who runs to the line of scrimmage. Next, the quarterback calls the play again and then breaks the team for the line.

The following are the hole numbers and the back numbers:

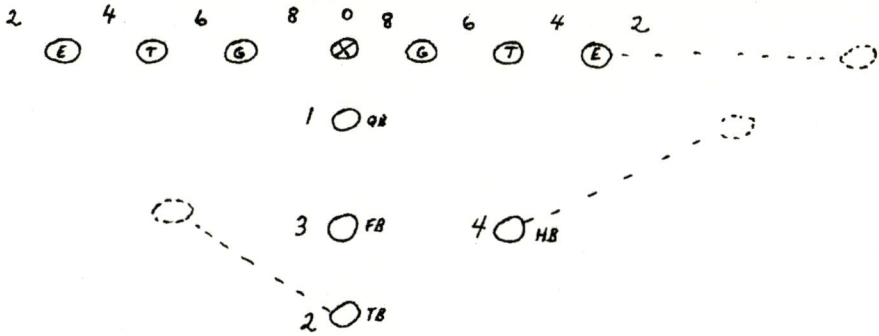

Note that the hole numbers are the same on both sides of the center for simplicity. The quarterback will call the formation to the right or left and the play to the right or left.

The following formations can be used, but others could be added by each individual coach.

{POWER I RT. OR LT.}

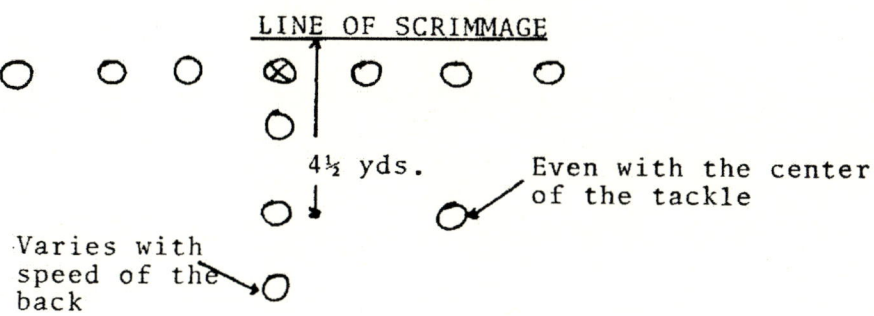

{I PRO RIGHT OR LEFT}

{I SLOT RIGHT OR LEFT}

{SLOT RIGHT OR LEFT}

{STRONG SLOT RIGHT OR LEFT}

{STRONG SLOT RT. OR LF. SPLIT}

RUNNING PLAYS

This list is the sets of series that can be run, but not all of these plays will be diagramed.

<u>Fly Series</u>
46 dive
34 slant
38 fly
22 fly

<u>Power Series</u>
34 power
26 sprint power
Fake 26 sprint power

<u>Cross Buck Series</u>
38 cross buck
46 cross buck

<u>Triple Option</u>
38 dive
triple option

Quarterback keep

<u>Wham and Counters</u>
38 dive
26 wham
20 counter
46 counter
30 quick trap

These running plays have pass plays attached to them that should be used in later games. They are: fake 22 fly pass at 8, Fake 46 cross buck pass at 4, fake 26 sprint pass at 2, triple option pass at 4, fake 20 counter drop back. These special plays should be unleashed in the first district game in which they are needed, and can be used as often as needed thereafter. The key to offense is to run the same rushing play as long as it gets four yards; when the defense stops it, then run that play to the opposite side. If the defense stops that play, then run the passing series. Each coach will learn how to mix his plays with experience. Also, running to the left and right sides equally will come with experience.

The next diagrams are for the special series plays and a random sample of others. The special plays are only run after the series has been run several times.

SPECIAL PLAYS

{ST. SLOT RT. FAKE 22 FLY RT. PASS AT 8 RT.}

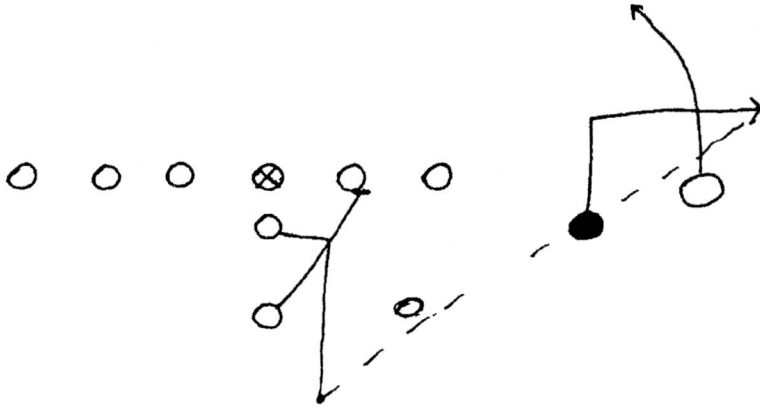

{POWER I RT. FAKE 46 X BUCK LT. PASS AT 4 RT.}

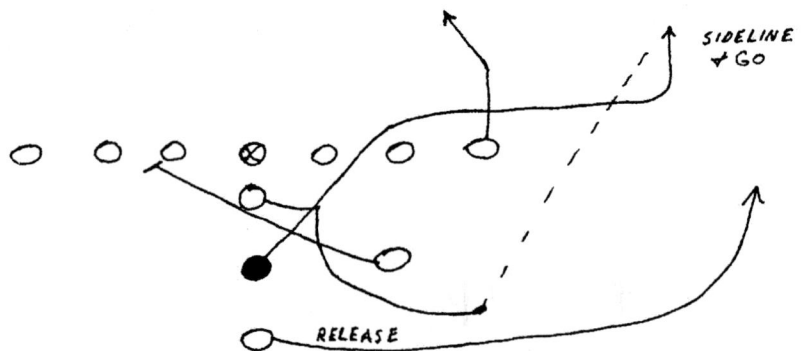

This is the Bread and Butter Play. QB may run with tailback blocking, throw to tailback or end, but primarily may throw to the fullback in the flat or deep. If the QB does a pump fake, then that tells the fullback to go deep for the bomb.

SPECIAL PLAYS

{PRO I RT. FAKE 26 SPRINT POWER RT PASS AT 2 RT.}

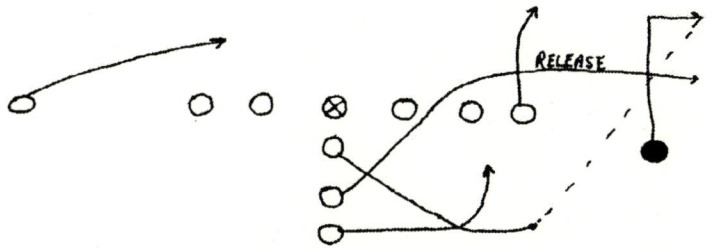

{SLOT RT. FAKE TRIPLE OPTION RT. PASS AT 4 RIGHT}

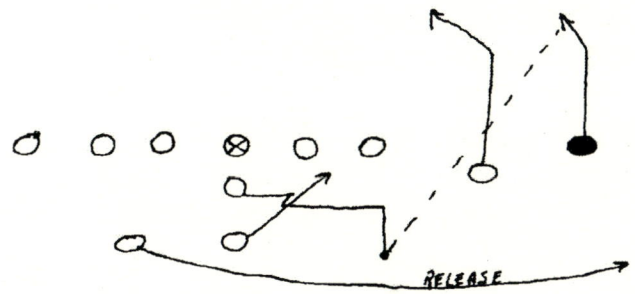

{I PRO RT. FAKE 20 COUNTER LT.   DROPBACK PASS}

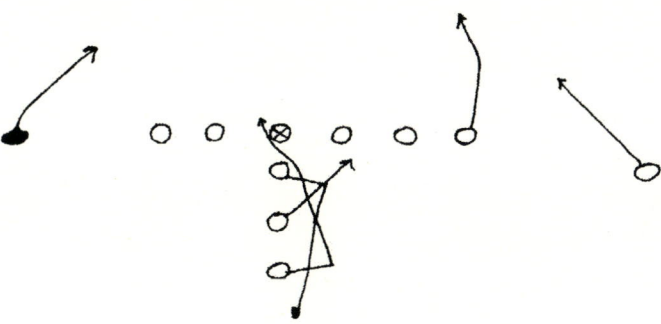

FLY SERIES

{ST. SLOT RT. 46 DIVE RT.}

{ST. SLOT RT. 34 SLANT RT.}

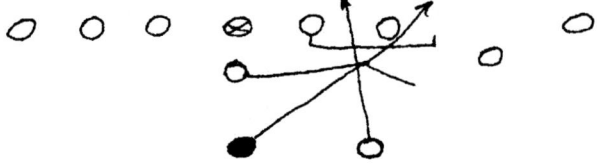

{ST. SLOT RT. 38 FLY RT.   FAKE PITCH FIRST}

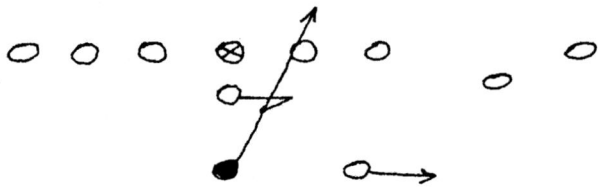

ST. SLOT RT. 22 FLY

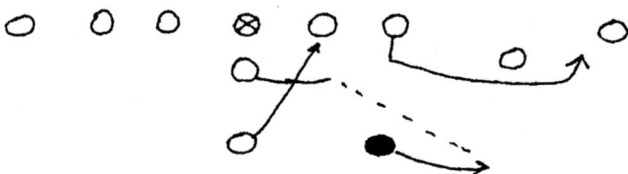

SERIES PLAYS
POWER SERIES
{I SLOT RT.   34   POWER RT.}

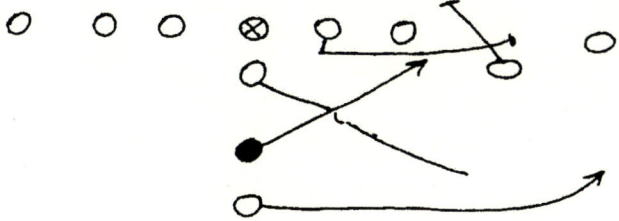

{I SLOT RT.   26 SPRINT POWER RT.}

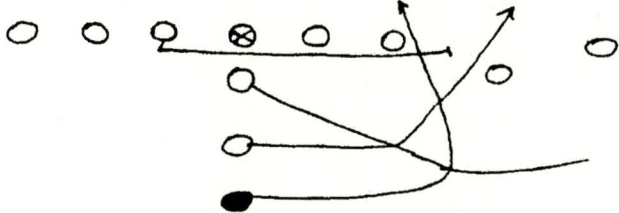

{I SLOT RT.   FAKE 26 SPRINT POWER RT. QB KEEP}

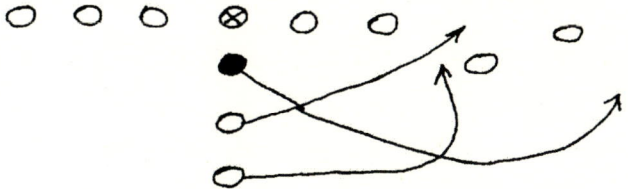

CROSS OR X BUCK SERIES
{POWER I RT.   38 X BUCK RT.}

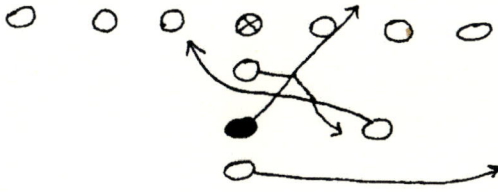

{POWER I RT. 46 X BUCK LT.}

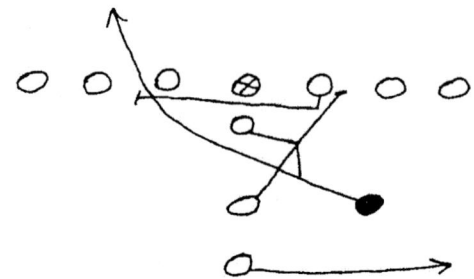

TRIPLE OPTION SERIES
{SLOT RT. 38 DIVE RT.}

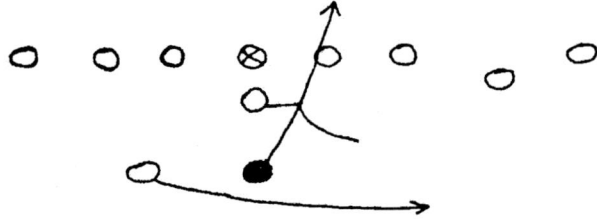

{SLOT RT. TRIPLE OPTION RT. PITCH KEEP OR GIVE}

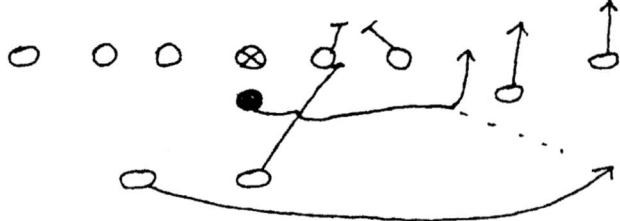

The Right Way to Coach Football

{WHAMS AND COUNTER SERIES
POWER I RT. WHAM RT.}

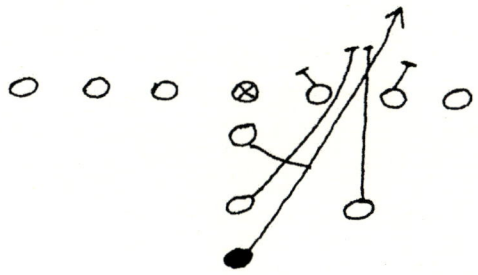

{POWER I RT. 30 COUNTER TRAP}

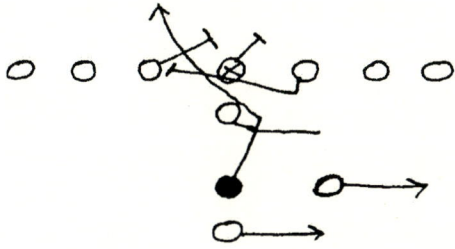

{POWER I RT. 20 COUNTER}

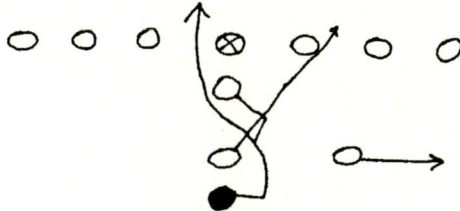

{ST. SLOT RT. 46 COUNTER LT.   (X BUCK FROM POWER I)}

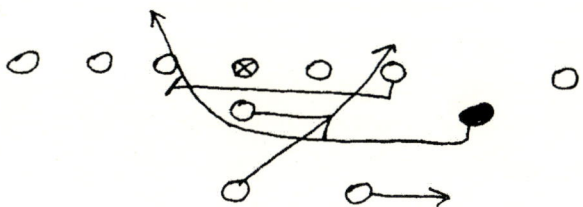

This running game is designed to fake defenses and to show different looks. Most plays can also be run to the left from the same formation and this should be done to give a balanced attack. The quarterback should be a smooth ball handler and intelligent. Coaches must brief quarterbacks on the total system because the quarterback calls everything that needs to be done. It is not important that other players learn the whole system, and this means fewer mistakes. Every school has a few intelligent quarterbacks, but sometimes an effort must be made to find them. A quarterback should be tall and quick if possible. A coach can develop a tall quarterback.

Ball-handling is very important and should be taught. Most quarterbacks need to balance their weight equally on both feet and not stand so close to the center. The center should put a little forward weight on the ball so that he must take a step when the snap is gone in order to keep from falling face down. The quarterback should make right-handed hand –offs with his right hand under the ball and left handed hand-offs with his left hand under the ball. Backs should raise their left elbow for a right side pocket and the right elbow for a left side pocket.

All backs should be taught who the key blocks are on each play and should run accordingly. Examples are pulling guards or tackles and fullbacks on whams. Backs need to be quick to run off these blocks or run over these blockers if they do not get out of the way.

Against stunting defenses, linemen should be taught to carry their man in the direction he is going. A good back must pick up this move, and hit the seams of this stunting defense. It is easy for an offensive lineman to take a stunter completely out of the play if he keeps his feet and moves the stunter in the direction his momentum is carrying him. On occasions where stunting is hurting the offense, the coach should call wedge-blocking at the hole the play is called. Linemen line up foot-to-foot and wedge at the hole. This can also be sued on short yardage situations. The quarterback calls the play on down or "on three" to confuse the defense. Plays like whams and dives can be called, and the offense will have to bind together to ground out the yardage. Quick passes to either end will also be used in short yardage situations.

BLOCKING RULES

All slants, powers and the 46 cross buck will be trap plays with a double team as a key block for the backs to run. These will be worked on at daily practice scrimmages. Other rules are as simple as counting from one to three.

<u>The Centers</u>
1. Blocks number 0 which is a lineman on the line of scrimmage directly in front of the center.
2. Checks play side linebacker if two linebackers are present without a nose guard. If the linebacker comes in the center blocks him, if not the center blocks the off side linebacker.
3. On dives and whams, he will block the nose guard or the offside linebacker.

<u>The Guards</u>
1. Will block number one man past the center.
2. On whams and 50 passes, he will block number one man on the line of scrimmage.
3. On whams will double with the center if a nose guard is present.
4. Backside guard will hinge block on all 50 passes and block aggressive block on sprint passes. A hinge block is a passive block that beckons the defender to come in and then hit him. it is done by dropping the outside foot back and pivoting on the inside foot.

<u>The Tackles</u>
1. Blocks the second man past the center.
2. Blocks the second man on the line of scrimmage on whams and fifty passes.
3. Backside tackle will hinge block on all 50 passes and aggressive block on sprint passes.

<u>The Ends</u>
1. Block the third man from the center.
2. Double team with tackle on powers and slants.
3. Backside end bumps his man and goes down field to block.

The following are special blocking assignments:

The offside tackle pulls on 46 counter and on 22 fly. He will block the first defender that shows at the hole of the play and go down field to block if no one is present. The offside guard pulls on 30 counter, 34 slant, and 26 sprint power, and does the same thing that the tackle does. Many coaches have special plays they may add, but this plan shows a good sample of these plays.

A few more things to remember about the offensive line-- tackles and guards never go down field on passing plays. This will telegraph a run to the defensive back, and he will come up to make the tackle with reckless abandon. Normal splits for linemen will be two feet from the center for guards and three feet from the guards for the tackles. Ends will be three feet from the tackles unless split wide. The formation called tells the end whether or not he is to split.

The fullbacks will be four and one half yards from the line of scrimmage and the tailback will be no more than one yard behind the fullback. The tailback is the only man to be in a two-point stance with his hands on his knees. Halfbacks will line up at fullback level directly behind the tackles. The slotbacks or pro backs line up two yards behind the line of scrimmage.

PASSING PLAYS OTHER THAN PLAY ACTION

All dropbacks are called "fifty floods." We also run sprint passes at two and four right or left.

PASSING DIAGRAMS

ST. SLOT RT.   50 PASS   A RT.

Fullbacks check linebacker, end and releases on all 50 passes. More routes can be run like circles, hooks and sidelines. Call them 50 D E F. Don't forget the release man if everyone is covered.

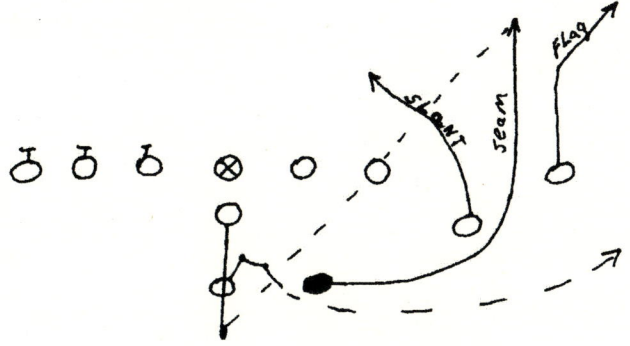

ST. SLOT RT.   50 PASS   B RT.
Slotback takes a 1001, 1002 delay Yells hot if the linebacker blitz is on. Quarterback will quickly throw to the slotback in this case.

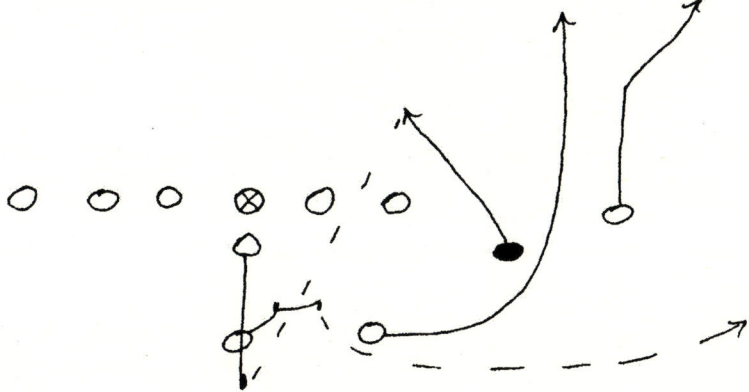

ST. SLOT RT. 50 PASS C RT.

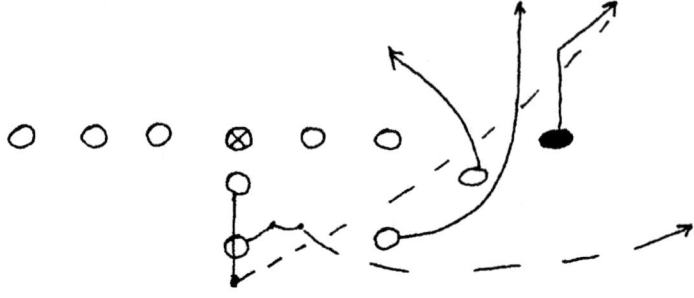

I PRO RT. SPRINT PASS AT 4 RT.

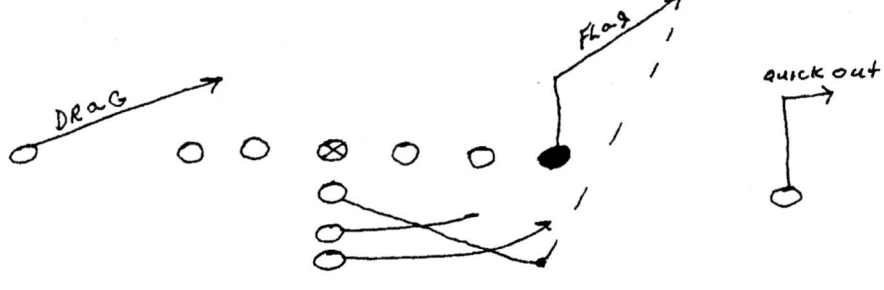

I PRO RT. SPRINT PASS AT 2 RT.
A Good Play When the Clock Is Running Down

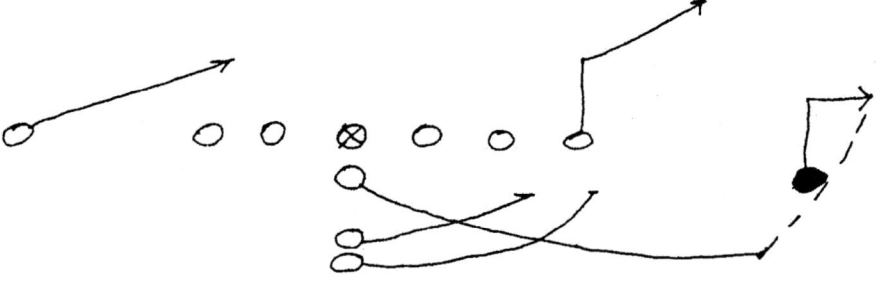

I PRO RT. SPRINT PASS AT 4 RT. THROWBACK LT.

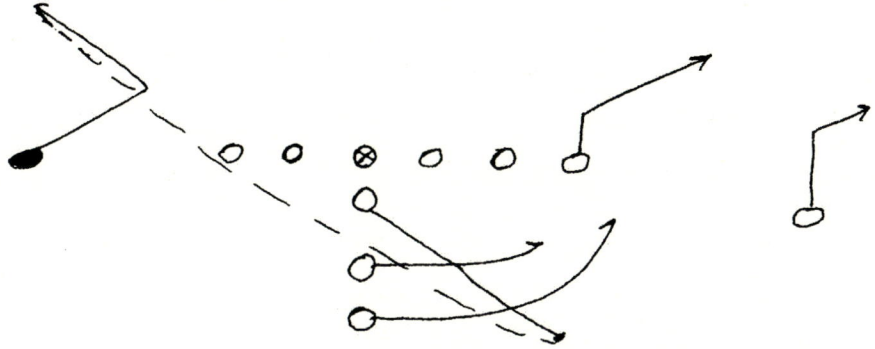

To conclude the offense, be sure to prepare quarterbacks and wide receivers on audibles. The team is given the live numbers before the game. If, at any time the quarterback feels that one of the wide receivers can get open, he calls the live number. Examples are as follows: Split end's number is 82--this means that the live numbers for him will be 81 and 83. If 83 is called, he runs a quick out; if 81 is called, he runs a quick slant in and the quarterback gets the ball to him. The quarterback is responsible to call cover to his teammates on all passes in the flat; this prevents touchdowns from interceptions.

The offensive plays drawn can all be run from the left side. A coach should remember to call plays to the backside for balance. The diagrams that have been shown are a sample, and many more could be added. It is suggested that a coach should select two series per game along with the passes and this should be enough to win most games.

Winning also depends on the ability of the players, but once a winning tradition is started it is easy to keep it going. Coaches must have high scoring offenses and must work on the short yardage plays every day to punch the ball across the goal every time opportunity knocks.

A coach must realize that each error can cause a score. Errors will be made on defense because there are eleven possibilities for error. Most coaches agree that you must have the best eleven players on defense to win consistently, but it is also true that the best players are needed on offense, especially offensive linemen. So, get the offense perfected, then worry about the defense. It comes along more naturally than offense because it relies mostly on instinct.

DEFENSE

In order to be efficient on defense, one must teach players how to read keys, how to react quickly, play responsibilities first, then pursue the football. Many coaches teach stunting techniques immediately, and the player gets to a point where he thinks he needs to depend on stunts. This causes one to lose confidence. Stunts are needed at times, but only when absolutely necessary.

I always did favor the 5 – 4 defense because it is good against the outside run with two cornerbacks, and it is good against the pass with two good middle linebackers. I will be illustrating this defense for my purposes in this system. Other defenses often used are the 4 – 4 when linebackers are small and need to be shielded by down linemen; or the split six when one has an abundance of big down lineman type players. The wide tackle six is used also, but not many teams have tacklers who are fast enough for it, because tackles must contain on this defense. This means they have to catch fast backs before the back turns up the field on end sweeps. The ends drop back on pass coverage which makes the tackle's job a lot more difficult. If a coach chooses one of these other defenses, he can find out a lot about them at coaching clinics; however, the main difference in defenses is some are odd man fronts and others are even man fronts. The split six has the middle open with guards over the offensive guards. The 4 – 4 has linebackers stacked behind down linemen in the gaps between the center and the guards.

The 5 – 4 will be illustrated throughout the rest of this section, but remember, there are many others. In my opinion, the 5 – 4 is hard to beat. The 5 – 4 is made of a strong nucleus triangle in the middle, composed of a nose guard and two linebackers. A coach can find the three strongest and quick men on the team for these spots, and the defense will work.

The following illustrations will show alignment of the 5 – 4 against various offenses. 0 = Offense; ^ = Defense

{5 - 4 ZONE}

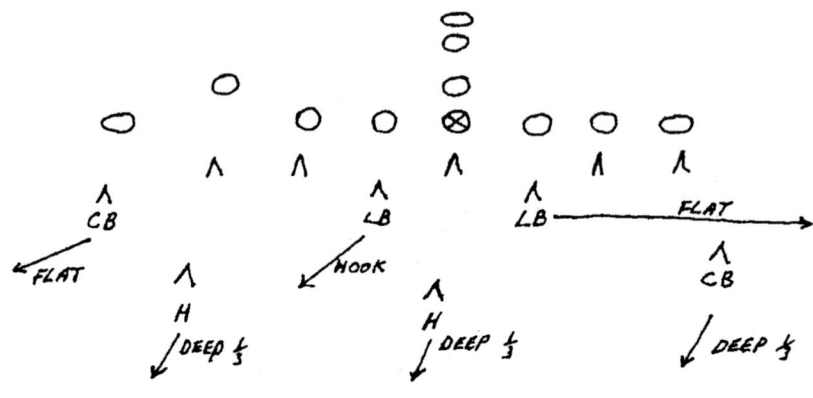

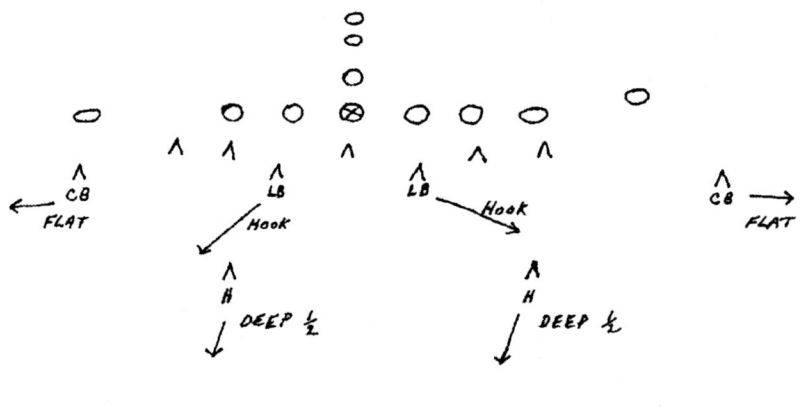

{ZONE}

The Right Way to Coach Football

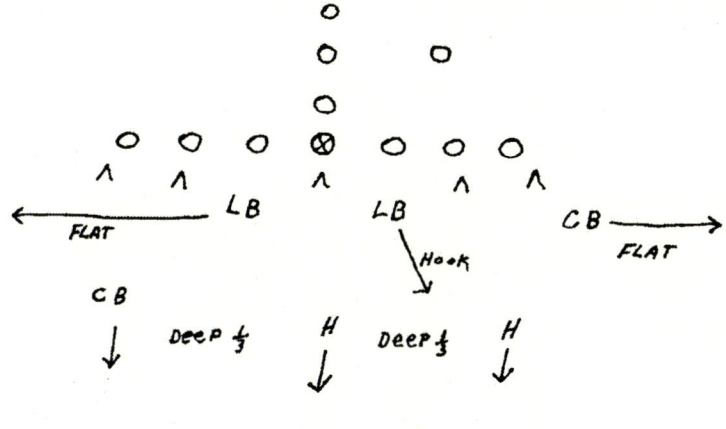

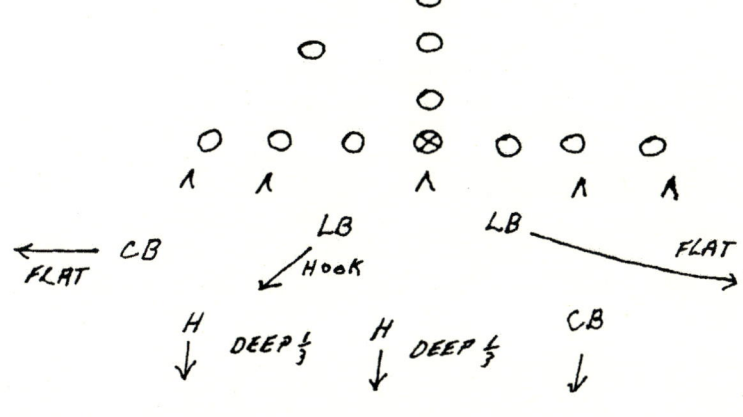

{5-4 MAN TO MAN}

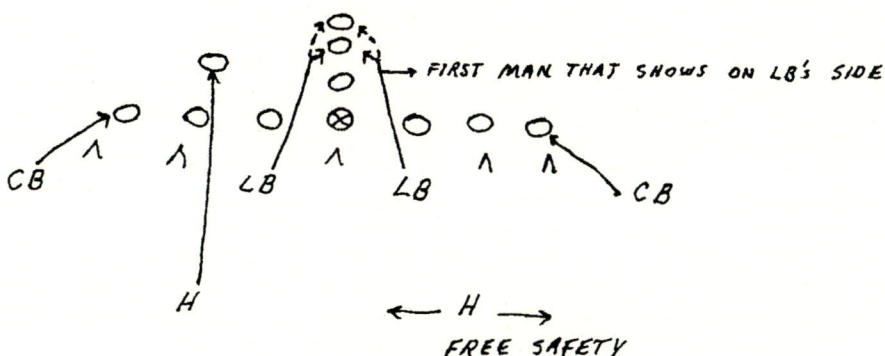

{5 - 4 MAN TO MAN}

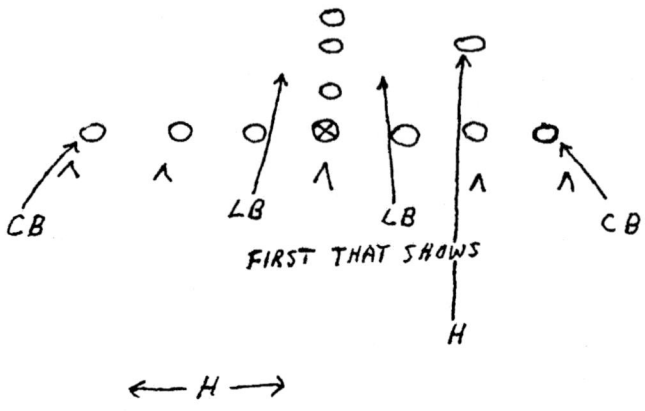

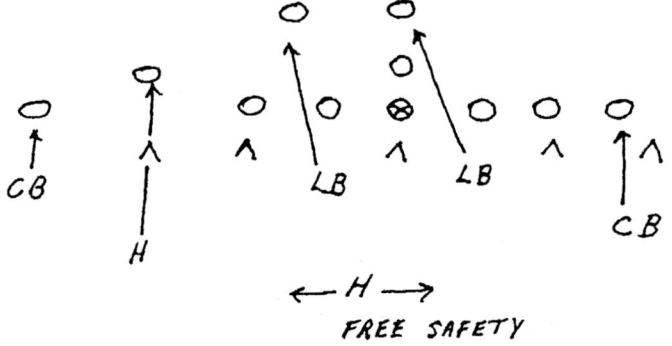

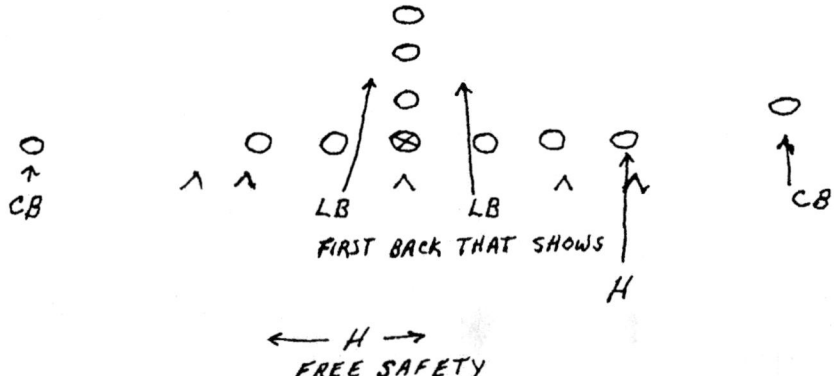

MAN TO MAN

```
                        O
                        O
       O            O
  O              O  O  ⊗  O    O
  ↑  ↑         ∧  ∧  ↑  ↑  ∧  ∧    ↑
  CB            LB        LB       CB
   ↑                                
   H         ← H →
            FREE SAFETY
```

{ON THIS TYPE OF OFFENSIVE SET MAN TO MAN IS A MUST.}

The zone is a simple rotation to the strong side and covers the respective areas. The man to man is strictly what the term implies; the general rule on the zone is the halfbacks are not to let anyone get behind them. Their first step is back. On man to man, it is not a step back, but a step toward the offensive man. The zone is good against tight offensive sets. Man to man is good against wide offensive sets.

5 - 4 ZONES FOR DEFENSIVE BACKS

(A) <u>Alignment</u>
Defensive line up 7 yards off the ball, head up with the offensive tackles. The outside foot is staggered, and the first move is one step back.

(B) <u>Keys</u>
Defensive backs should look at the offensive tackle's move, if the tackle comes down the field then immediately come up on the running play because no interior lineman can go down field on a pass play. If the tackle stays on the line of scrimmage, then the back should drop back, read the quarterback and go to the football.

(C) <u>Technique</u>

The back must be in a two point stance with knees bent and must react quickly to the pass or run. He must not dive at any ball carrier, but tackle him high at shoulder level. He should always play receivers by looking at his mid section because it cannot make a fake. Halfbacks should always give fast receivers a lot of cushion and never let receivers get behind him or behind any other defensive back. When the ball is thrown, go to it, not the receiver.

5 – 4 CORNERBACKS

(A) <u>Alignment</u>
Two to four yards off of the ball, outside foot staggered. If the end is tight with no pro back play one yard outside of the offensive end. If the end splits more than 3 yards go with him, but line up on his inside, because the side line helps on an outside pattern. If a pro back comes out, split the difference between him and the end.

(B) <u>Keys</u>
Use peripheral vision to pick up receivers and quarterback; if receivers block, look for the run. If they go down field, then look of the pass in the flat. When cornerback rotates, he has safetyback duties. Cornerbacks must stop the outside sweeps and pitches first, then go to their passing zone.

(C) <u>Technique</u>
If a running play develops, he must come up quickly to force the run inside. On the option he has the pitch man. On pass he looks at the quarterback and reacts to the ball.

5 - 4 ZONE FOR LINEBACKERS

(A) <u>Alignment</u>
Two yards off of the ball and head up with the offensive guard. Feet parallel to the line of scrimmage.

(B) <u>Key</u>
Looks at guard's move first if guard pulls linebacker goes to the line of scrimmage and follows the guard, picking up the football and making the tackle. If the guard blocks down on the center,

linebacker charges in for a wham or trap play. If the guard blocks the linebacker, then get rid of the guard with hands and make the tackle. If the guard pass blocks or hingeblocks, the linebacker goes to the hook zone, if he is on the strong side of the offensive set. He goes to the flat zone if he is on the weak side of the offensive play. The linebacker picks up the action of the quarterback and goes to the football.

(C) <u>Technique</u>

When falling in to take on the wham, he must be tough and drop to all fours. Help should come from safeties and corners. If the guard comes out aggressive, read his block; don't let him get his headgear across your body. If he is trying to block you to your right, then hit him with a right forearm and go left, and vice versa. If the guard pass blocks, go to your zone or follow your man out of the backfield.

The zone defense will be used against tight sets, short yardage situations, or victory defense, but the man to man is a much better defense. Some coaches are hesitant to play man to man because the wide receivers are usually too fast, but there are ways to combat this. One way is a good pass rush and another way is to hit the receiver at the line of scrimmage.

5 - 4 MAN TO MAN

<u>Halfbacks or Defensive Backs</u>

(A) <u>Alignment</u>

Seven yards from the ball and head up with his receiver which is usually the tight end or the offensive halfback. Outside foot should be back on the stance.

(B) <u>Keys</u>

Follow his man and pick up the football through peripheral vision.

(C) <u>Technique</u>

Same as zone, except he doesn't take a step back

<u>Free Safety Halfbacks--may be designated as free safety on all plays.</u>

(A) <u>Alignment</u>

Seven yards from the football but can center himself between the offensive spread or go to an overloaded side such as a twin set. Outside foot is back.

(B) <u>Keys</u>

Uses football instinct to go to the ball or if one receiver is outstanding, he will double team that person. This back can make a lot of tackles when he suspects a running play and reads the quarterback's action.

(C) <u>Technique</u>

Same as zone except doesn't take one step back.

<u>Cornerbacks</u>

(A) <u>Alignment</u>

If the end stays tight, three yards from the tackle or less, then line up on the ends outside shoulder slightly. If the end splits out, line up on his outside shoulder until he gets close to the sideline, then line up on his inside shoulder. Do the same if a pro back splits out; leave the tight end for the halfback. Outside foot back.

(B) <u>Keys</u>

Play your man on pass plays; then go to the football. If your man is not split out very far, seven yards or more, then play him tight and hit him on the line of scrimmage and play the football. If the receiver is exceptional, hit him on the line of scrimmage at any position he may get into.

(C) <u>Technique</u>

Same as zone except cover your man on pass plays.

<u>Linebackers</u>

(A) <u>Alignment</u>

Same as zone, feet parallel to the line of scrimmage.

(B) <u>Keys</u>

Same as zone except follow first man out of the backfield to your side if it is a pass play.

(C) <u>Technique</u>

Same as zone defense

<u>Ends</u>

(A) <u>Alignment</u>

On the line of scrimmage, on the outside shoulder of the offensive end or slot back. Outside foot back. If end splits more than three feet, then stay inside of him. the same for slotbacks. Always us a two point stance. If the end splits more than three feet, then let him go and stay in close to your defensive tackle. The cornerback will go out with the receiver.

(B) <u>Key</u>

Look at ends move; don't let him hook you; keep your outside foot free at all times. If he tries to kick you out, force him in and make the tackle. If he tries to go out for a pass, hit him; then rush the passer.

(C) <u>Technique</u>

Use the inside forearm to hit the end every play, and use the outside arm for leverage to push the end toward the inside clogging off the tackle play. Use hands to get rid of blockers on outside plays, and keep the outside foot free. Rush the passer on all pass plays. Keep the end off balance so he cannot double-team on the defensive tackle.

Tackles

(A) <u>Alignment</u>

On the line of scrimmage with your nose on the outside shoulders of the offensive tackle. Four point stance should be used.

(B) <u>Key</u>

Read the offensive tackle and pick up the play. Push him into the guard if possible. If the end doubles on you, get on all fours and try to lift the two blockers. If you keep your position, you are doing your job.

(C) <u>Technique</u>

Fire out on the tackle with and inside forearm and use the other arm for leverage to push inward. If your man blocks down, get on all fours looking inside for a guard or fullback block.

Nose Guard

(A) <u>Alignment</u>

On the line of scrimmage, head up with center, Four point stance.

(B) <u>Keys</u>

Go to the opposite direction of the center's block, and use peripheral vision to see if guards are to double team. Find the quarterback, and go the football.

(C) <u>Technique</u>

Fire out on the center hard and square to the line of scrimmage. If the center is blocking you to your right, hit him with your right forearm and move to your left, and vice versa. On a double-team from the guards hit the ground on all fours and lift. If you can create a big pile, then you have done your job. On pass plays get rid of the center using the off hand for leverage and go to the quarterback.

The following diagrams are the angles that each player should take after they have performed their keys and responsibilities and the play went in another direction. 0 = Offense; ^ = Defense

{PURSUE ROUTES}

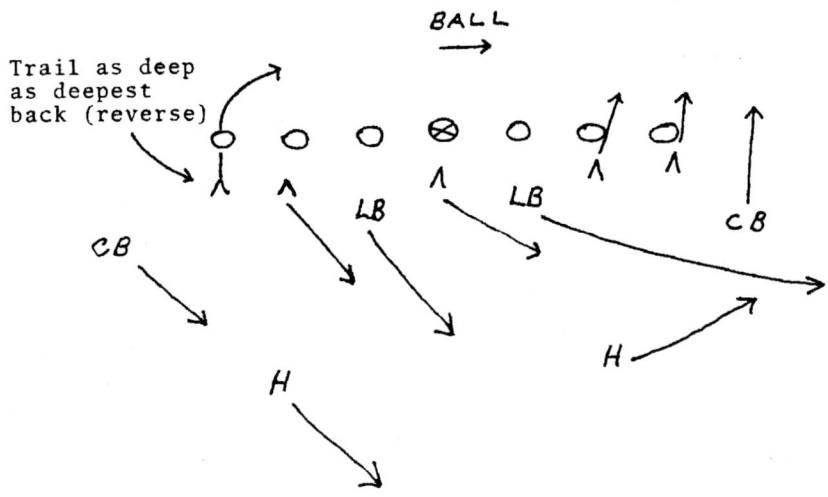

{PURSUE ROUTES}

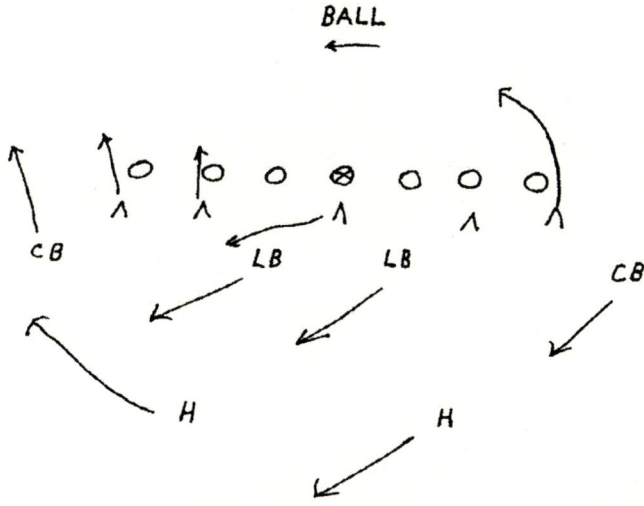

A preventive defense will be called on long yardage situations, and towards the end of the first half of the game when we are ahead. This can also be called a victory defense. The only adjustment needed are dropping halfbacks, linebacks and cornerbacks two to five yards deeper than their normal alignment. Play a zone defense on a pass play.

{VICTORY DEFENSE}

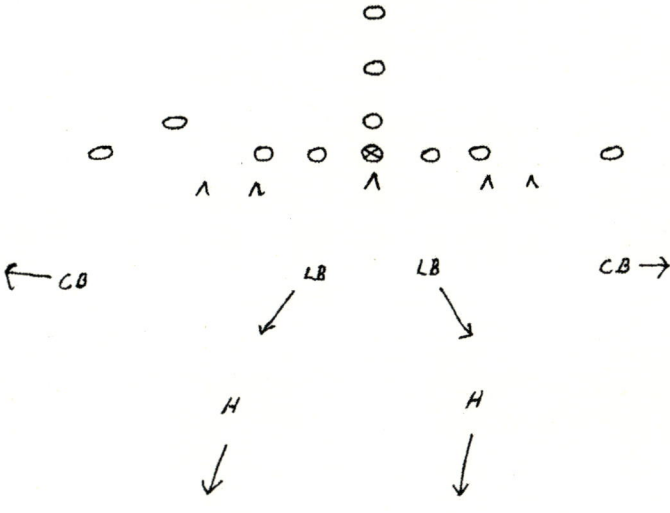

Goal line and short yardage defense will be a six-one. The down lineman will penetrate past the line of scrimmage to upset the backfield action. The backs will play a zone defense. The following diagrams will illustrate the action to be taken to the strongside of the offense and to the backside of the offense.

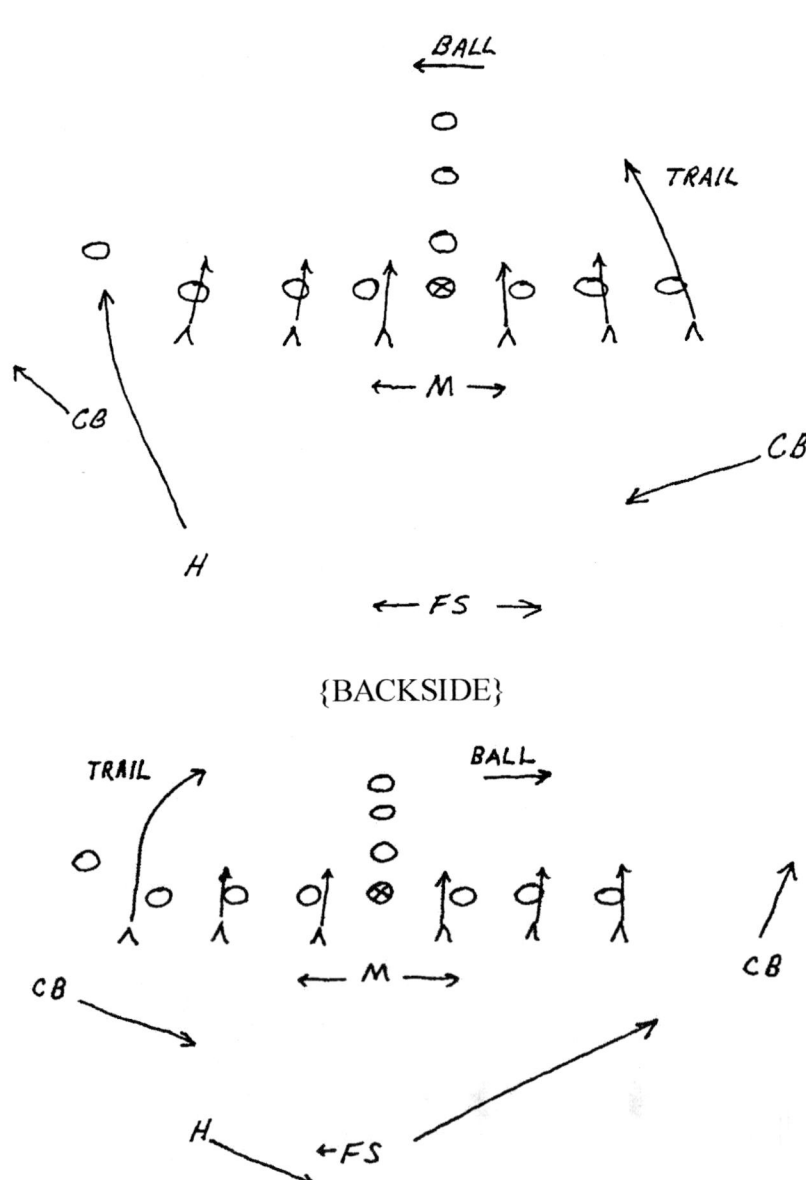

The Right Way to Coach Football

On dropback passes, the middle lineback will drop back to the center of the field and the other backs will go to their zones. See this diagram.

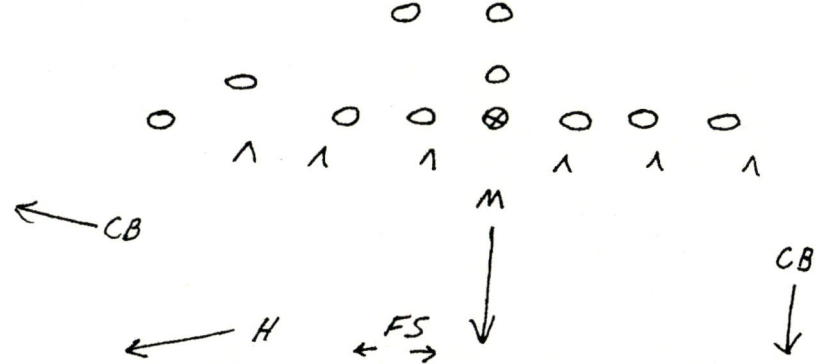

The free safety will line up where he can be in the center of the most receivers. If the six linemen are drilled to penetrate, then the defense will be successful.

This defense will work if coaches will teach alignment, keys, responsibilities, and techniques every day at the defensive time of the practice schedule. Players should be taught that everybody must pursue the ball after technique and keys have been checked. Stress one hundred percent on every play, and tell the defense that they must never stop until the whistle blows.

As mentioned before, this is only one defense, but it is very sound. If teams hurt the defense on long passes, then blitz the offside linebacker and tell ends to blitz, also. Ends should be getting to the quarterback on all dropback passes. Also, ends get quarterbacks on options and linebackers should be in the flats on end sweeps or pitches. If a team is hurting the defense on the running game, then call both tackles to pinch inside. This should help. Stunts can help, but they should not be a big part of the defensive strategy. It is wise to note that on man to man coverage the cornerbacks have a big job in chopping down wide receivers and picking them up on the pass play. Cornerbacks must be quick. Quickness and agility are the keys to defense, and the practice schedule certainly allows for this type of ability to be developed. If coaches will stress one hundred percent effort at all drills, then the defensive team will be efficient.

It is far more important to use every minute of practice going full speed, than it is to have people sitting around wasting time and getting sluggish. Reward the team if they have a snappy practice by shortening sprint time on various days. This will motivate them into going full speed in all drills. This will also develop good long lasting habits. Remember, it is important to keep all players happy, not just the first eleven.

Designate a linebacker to call shift right or left if the line is off balance. Some teams may have only two men on the line of scrimmage on one side of the center, and the other side of the center will have four men. there should be three and three on each side of the center on the line of scrimmage in order to have a balanced line. Don't count the pro back; he is off of the line of scrimmage, but the split end is on the line of scrimmage. The linebacker will have to pick up unequal line ups and then let the team know how many positions to move and in what direction.

KICKING GAME

Every day before practice begins, centers, quarterbacks, holders, kickers, punters, and receivers should practice while others are dressing. At the end of scrimmage schedules, kick a few punts every day and return punts at the same time. On Thursday's or the day before the game, go over kicking teams and various wild offensive sets.

Linemen are to block inside and the three backs are to take one step up and block on all punts. Backs must step up because the punter might kick them. If a punter is left footed, then put two backs on the left side of the punter. All men cover at the sound of the punt. The punter must take only two steps during the punting technique. A right footed punter should have his right foot back at the start of the punt. His right foot moves forward first, then his left foot takes a step, then he kicks with the next step. The following diagrams will illustrate the punting formations, and the punt return formation and movements of the players.

{TIGHT PUNTING FORMATION}

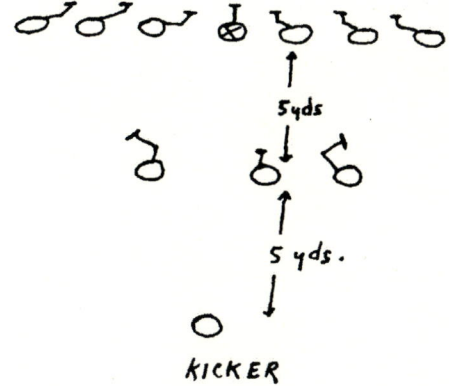

{PUNT RETURN RIGHT (JUST THE OPPOSTIE FOR THE LEFT}

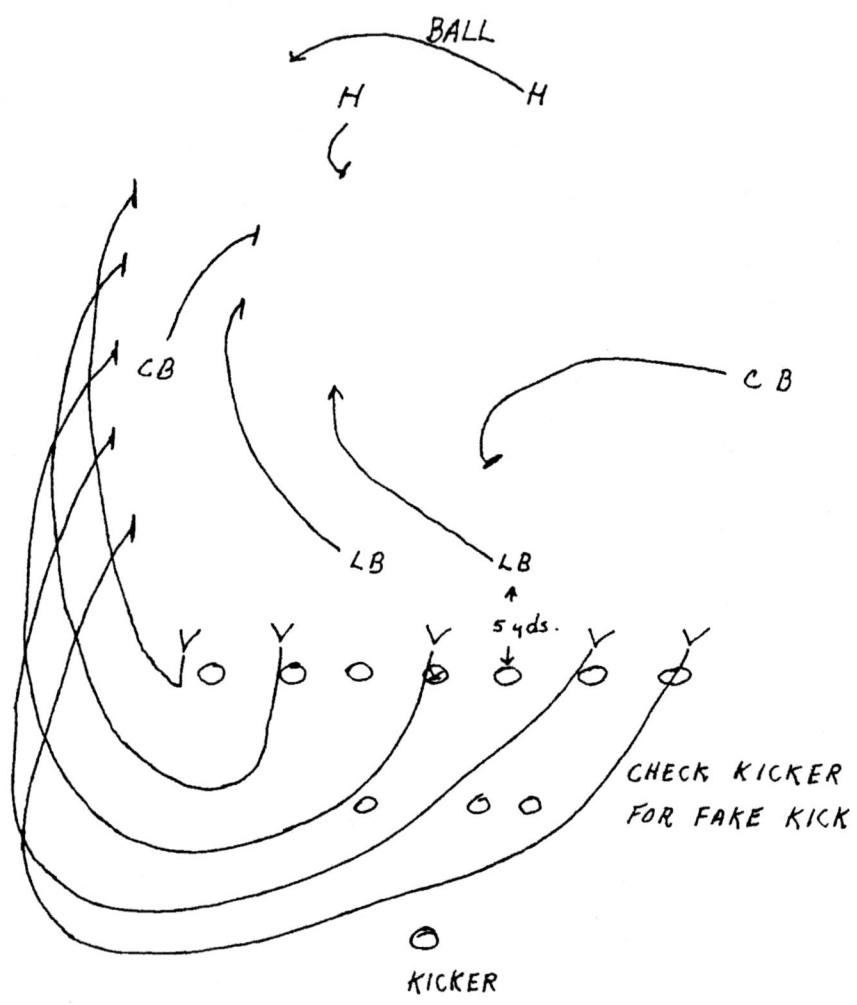

POINTERS FOR PUNT RECEIVING

If the punt is high and short, call a fair catch.
If the punt is past the ten-yard line, let it go.
On other punts, use your own judgment.
Try to get behind the wall of blockers. If this is impossible, run straight up the field and get what you can.

{K I C K O F F}

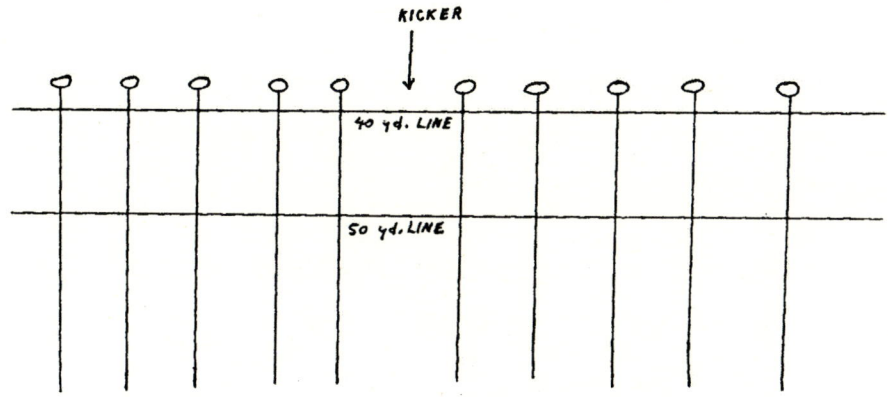

Stay in lanes until players reach the ball carrier.
Ball must go past the 50-yard line to be a legal kick.

{KICK OFF RETURN UP THE MIDDLE}

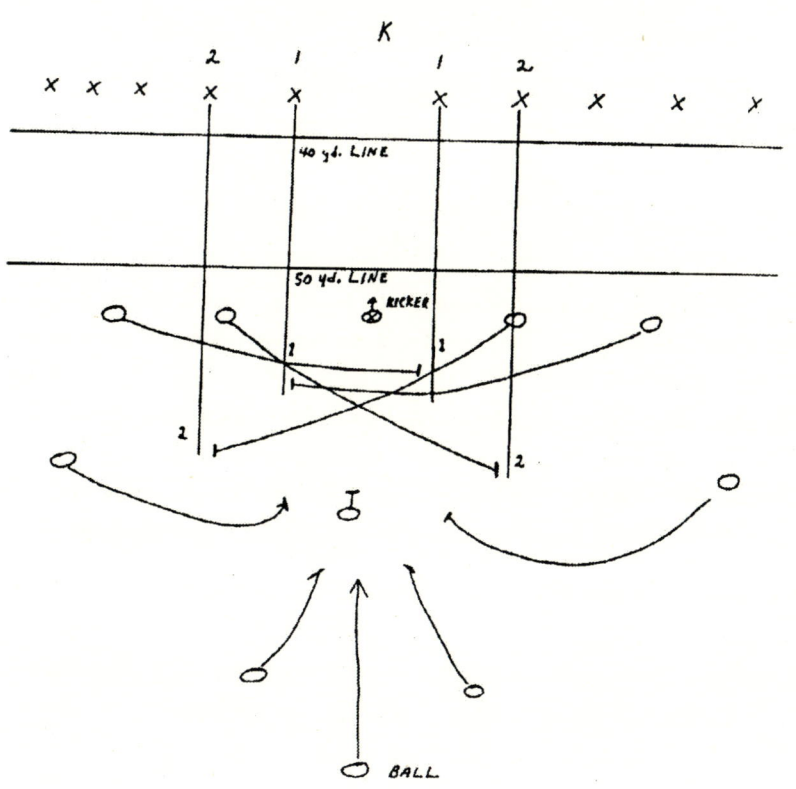

{KICK OFF RETURN RIGHT, SAME TO THE LEFT}

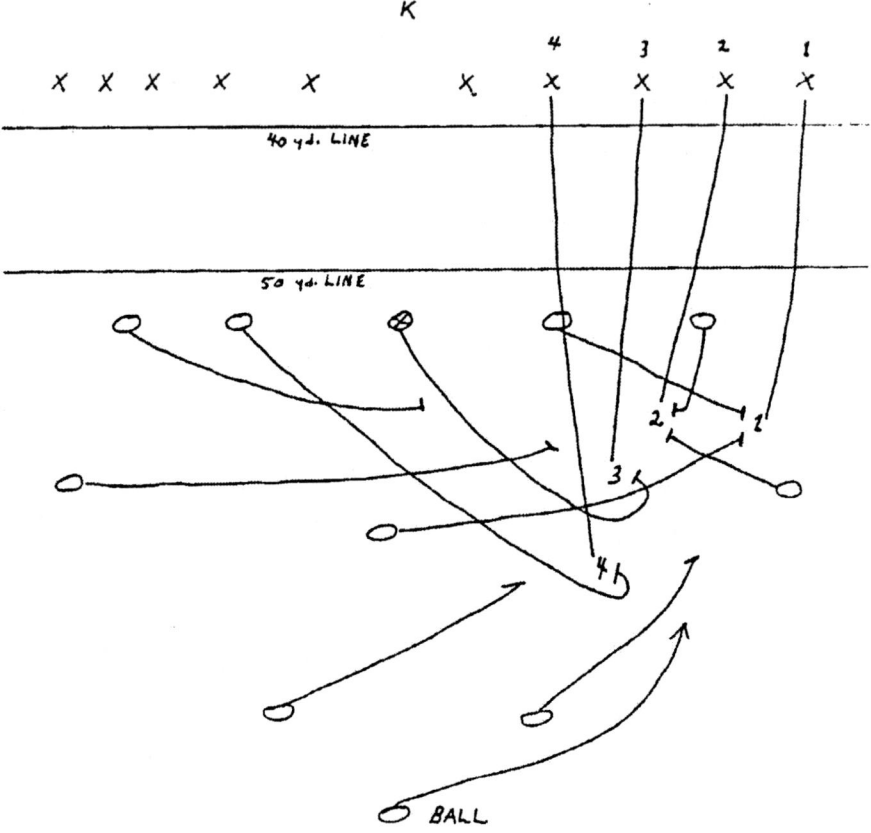

The kickoff returns are easy to run. Up the middle, let the guards and tackles count 1 and 2 respectively on the opposite side of the kicker, and that will be the man he blocks. On the return right, the counting is from the end toward the kicker. The fullback and right guard double on number one defender; the tackle and end double on the number two defender. The center gets number three, and the left guard gets number four. These returns can be very effective if practiced and timing is perfected.

SUMMARY

Points to remember are that safety and human dignity must come first. Organization is the key and physical development is a must. The offense is such that the quarterback must do most of the thinking, and the plays are easy to follow. The defense is straight football that depends on teamwork and one hundred percent effort at all times.

Keeping the team happy by playing all members is very important. Work on each facet of the game every day at practice. Pick out two series of plays for each game, and work on these by briefing quarterbacks daily. The offense is designed to fake defenses. Pass plays should flood zones to assure success. The defense covers every play, and the practice schedule develops agility and quickness.

If anyone would like more details on any of this work, please contact the author at 40487 Cannon Road, Gonzales, Louisiana, 70737. I will be glad to correspond with anyone promoting the same goals that I have pointed out. This is not intended to be a complete football system, but it is thorough and flexible so that others can add to it. Drills and techniques can be illustrated on the football field, and I would be happy if anyone would need such demonstrations because I could help in this facet.

ABOUT THE AUTHOR

The author was born in 1946 in the small town of Sorrento, Louisiana, and spent all of his life in South Louisiana. He was a high school football standout, and earned a full football scholarship at Southeastern Louisiana University, Hammond, Louisiana in 1964. He earned three letters in football at Southeastern and graduated in Agricultural business in 1969. He then coached 10 years of junior high school and senior high school football. During the ten years of coaching the author attended many coaching conventions and kept notes of these conventions. He then decided to write this booklet because he had seen much abuse given out by many coaches, and this caused him to write this much needed booklet. He also covers every aspect of the game because on his first coaching job he didn't know how to begin, The booklet was written in 1985, but still stands today as a usable coaching guide for anyone interested in the game.

Printed in the United States
39884LVS00005B/196-198